In Our Own Voice

Poems by Odia Women Poets

In Our Own Voice

Poems by Odia Women Poets

Translated by
J. P. Das

Edited with an Introduction by
Vinita Gupta Chaturvedi

BLACK EAGLE BOOKS
Dublin, USA | Bhubaneswar, India

 Black Eagle Books
USA address:
7464 Wisdom Lane
Dublin, OH 43016

India address:
E/312, Trident Galaxy, Kalinga Nagar,
Bhubaneswar-751003, Odisha, India

E-mail: info@blackeaglebooks.org
Website: www.blackeaglebooks.org

First International Edition Published by
Black Eagle Books, 2023

IN OUR OWN VOICE
(Poems by Odia Women Poets)

Translated by **J. P. Das**

Edited with an Introduction by **Vinita Gupta Chaturvedi**

Translation Copyright © **J. P. Das**

All rights reserved. No part of this publication may be reproduced, stored in a retrieval system, or transmitted, in any form or by any means, electronic, mechanical, photocopying, recording or otherwise without the prior permission of the publisher.

Cover & Interior Design: Ezy's Publication

ISBN- 978-1-64560-429-7 (Paperback)
Library of Congress Control Number: 2023945054

Printed in the United States of America

CONTENTS

Introduction / Vinita Gupta Chaturvedi   9

My Whole Life for Him /
Manorama Mahapatra (Biswal)   21
So Many Days / Bijoyini Das   22
Ask Me / Bijoyini Das   24
Coincidence / Jyotsna Das   25
Dharmapada / Yashodhara Das   26
Murderer / Mamata Dash   28
On My Own Grave / Banaja Devi   30
To The Bird / Banaja Devi   31
Magician / Shakuntala Devi   32
Before Anyone Comes / Pravasini Mahakud   33
Father / Pravasini Mahakud   36
Don't Know Why / Pravasini Mahakud   37
Wherever You Are, Whichever Way You Go /
Pravasini Mahakud   38
The Last Man / Sanghamitra Mishra   40
Sorrow / Sanghamitra Mishra   42
Time's Other Name / Sanghamitra Mishra   44
The Sea / Yashodhara Mishra   46
Midnight Train / Yashodhara Mishra   47
Untitled / Aparna Mohanty   48
The Drain / Brahmotri Mohanty   51
Good News Bad News / Giribala Mohanty   52
Wherever You Are / Giribala Mohanty   52

Woman / Giribala Mohanty	55
You Forgot That / Giribala Mohanty	57
The Pedlar / Nirmala Mohanty	58
I Knew / Nirmala Mohanty	60
Wife/Mistress / Sasmita Mohanty	62
Tomorrow / Amiyabala Muni	64
My Mother is Smiling Today / Sulekha Samantaray	65
Rain Comes / Sarojini Sarangi	67
The Falklands / Pratibha Satpathy	68
Heroine / Pratibha Satpathy	69
The Oyster / Pratibha Satpathy	71
Eclipsed Time / Pratibha Satpathy	73
The Tryst / Sunanda Tripathy	75
Poem in Motion / Sunanda Tripathy	77
The Sweet-Smelling Earth / Sunanda Tripathy	78
Mirror / Bhagyalipi Malla	79
The Summit / Bhagyalipi Malla	80
Hide And Seek / Bhagyalipi Malla	81
Farmer's Song / Chirashree Indrasingh	82
That Night / Chirashree Indrasingh	84
The Blue Saree / Sucheta Mishra	85
Love / Sucheta Mishra	86
Boon / Swapna Mishra	87
Darling Daughter / Swapna Mishra	88
A Time to Speak Out / Madhuri Panda	90
Till Then / Madhuri Panda	91
In Silence / Sharmistha Sahu	92
Flight / Sharmistha Sahu	92
Chiaroscuro / Sharmistha Sahu	94
Shower at Sunset / Subhashree Lenka	95
Come this Night / Subhashree Lenka	96
Once You've Donned the Poet's Garb / Subhashree Lenka	98
Woman / Subhashree Lenka	100
Your Hand / Subhashree Lenka	102

Poetry / Pritidhara Samal	103
Sunday / Pritidhara Samal	105
Chess Board / Pratiksha Jena	107
Ahalya / Pratiksha Jena	108
Sunlight / Pratiksha Jena	109
Truth Untruth / Ipsita Sarangi	110
Born a Woman / Ipsita Sarangi	111
If You Meet a Poet / Sunanda Pradhan	112
Holi / Sunanda Pradhan	113
To the Seashore / Sunanda Pradhan	114
Looking at the Sea / Sunanda Pradhan	115
Violence / Gayatribala Panda	117
Tiger / Gayatribala Panda	119
Country / Gayatribala Panda	121
No One Comes / Srustishree Nayak	123
Home / Srustishree Nayak	124
Beloved's Life / Prabasini Hota	126
To My Pallbearers / Subhashree Subhasmita Mishra	128
Sentry / Sasmita Rout	129
Deity / Sasmita Rout	130
Colours of Words / Tanmayee Rath	131
Failed Assassin / Tanmayee Rath	132
Mask / Swapnajita Sankhua	134
Acknowledgements	135
Notes on the Poets	136

INTRODUCTION

Odisha has enjoyed a symbiotic relationship with poetry and has had a long and unbroken tradition of women writing poetry. Women have made significant contribution to the canon of Odia poetry, starting from the fifteenth century to the present. Among women poets of Odisha, perhaps the earliest is Madhabi Dasi, an exponent of Bhakti poetry and a contemporary of Sri Chaitanya. She wrote in Brajboli, Bangla and Odia. Her *janāna* "Chakānayan he Jagujiban Srihari" was one of her most popular devotional songs in Odia. *Nandabai Chautiśā* is another well-known poem composed by a woman from Odisha in pre-colonial times. Several women, mostly from royal families, composed devotional songs and long narrative poems in the eighteenth and nineteenth centuries.

Odisha witnessed a burst of feminine creative energy in the wake of Indian Independence which continued undiminished through the last quarter of the century and has reached a fruition in the present, when writing poetry has become almost *de rigeur*, where poetry reading sessions and publication have become a state-wide quotidian activity. *In Our Own Voice: Poems by Odia Women Poets* is an ambitious enterprise of the renowned poet, writer and playwright J. P. Das who has painstakingly culled, collected, and translated the creative outpourings of some of these women set far apart in time but geographically rooted in the state. Some of these poems were edited and translated by Das earlier and appeared in two separate anthologies, titled *In Other Words* (2017) and *Under the Silent Sun* (1992). He co-edited the latter with the Chicago-based academician Arlene Zide. The present volume contains poems from these collections as well as many other young and vibrant voices. Originally written in Odia language and meticulously translated into English by Das, these poems belong to women writers spanning nearly half a century, who come from diverse walks of life. Some of them are working professionals who hail from the world of corporate and journalism; some are fulltime writers while there are contributions from others who seem to steal time to compose verses in the interstices of their domestic chores.

The poems in this volume are rich and eclectic, which range over a variety of subjects, providing a polyphony of voices and a panoply of themes. The writers in this collection straddle different worlds-a little more than five decades separate Banaja Devi and Amiyabala Muni who were born in pre-independent India circa 1941, from the youngest contributors, Tanmayee Rath and Swapnajita Sankhua, born during the pre-reform and post-liberalisation period of India, in the years 1987 and 1998 respectively. Poems collected from such a broad time spectrum would naturally bring an array of thematic concerns and preoccupations. A brief overview of the development of Odia poetry by women over the decades since India's Independence would reveal that, like all women's poetry elsewhere in the world, there is a sense of thwarted aspiration and patriarchal oppression in the early set of poets, sometimes coupled with the mildest influence of western modernism, resulting in occasional experimentation. So, we have Jyotsna Das's abstruse simile in 'Coincidence', evocative of Yeats's fearsome beast in 'No Second Coming':

> The camel resting on the desert sands
> Rises, slowly moving
> Towards a sudden liberation.

Or the brutality of patriarchal exploitation which reduces the humiliated wife of 'Untitled' to "some fresh cut of meat" or the docile wife of 'Wife/Mistress', robbed of agency, reduced to:

> A small well
> Full of sweet cold water
> Whenever you need it,
> There to quench your thirst

The poetry of the Seventies and Eighties marked a move away from experimentation, drawing more upon the rich native tradition, folklore and myth. This departure is reflected in Sanghamitra Mishra's poetry, either when she is invoking the mythological characters in 'Time's Other Name' or when she is sympathising with the onerous, ordinary life of the deprived, the disenfranchised in 'The Last Man' :

> …that last man
> The voiceless pain of waiting
> When will he reach the Liongate-
> Of the Jagannath temple
> When will he beg benevolence of the god
> At the end of the journey?

The poets writing in the post-liberalisation era find themselves in a social and cultural landscape very different from the earlier one and do not shy away from expressing their innermost thoughts. The times have become more progressive and conducive to the poetic treatment of intimate subjects and unarticulated desires. While the older set of writers is a little reticent in articulating it, often taking the personal to the transcendental, and couching the physical in the spiritual and the symbolic; there is a sense of abandonment and unrestrained outpouring of innermost feelings in the poems of the younger generation. The imagery becomes more suggestive and is expressed forcefully, with a new-found intensity. Subhashree Lenka's metaphors mark one of the boldest celebrations of physical intimacy comparable to Lawrentian symbolism. 'Shower at Sunset' may ostensibly appear as a nature poem with an evocative description of the rains washing away the grime of the earth but the house on which it falls is a metaphor for the hermetic human body where passions lay dormant for long. Its parched innards are finally quenched in deeply sensuous images:

> The shower at sunset
> opened the doors of the house
> lying locked and neglected for ages
> and shattered its silence.
> It stepped unto the darkness
> Of the abandoned place,
> where lay trapped in time
> emptiness, loneliness
> and many forgotten passions.

The alliteration in the line where the rain restores "fervour of flight to the fatigued fledgling" is deeply suggestive of slumbering passions and a passionate awakening.

The poetry of the younger lot reflects an assured sense of confidence, self-reflection, and empowerment. Most of these writers must have reached their creative acme during the last decade of the millennium hence the selection of subjects is vast and varied but with a ring of contemporary relevance. Some of their writings are suffused with love and desire, are an exploration and celebration of the body and portray an uninhibited awareness of sexuality. In 'Come this Night' Lenka once again deploys quasi-religious imagery to celebrate the union of bodies. In a cascade of sensuous and erotic metaphors, the poem hurtles towards the climactic crescendo when the lovers unite in a joyous mingling of " blood, marrow, flesh, nerve and bone". 'Sunlight' and 'Sunday' are an expose on women's new-found freedom while 'Flight' rebels against women's circumscribed lives, defiantly resisting the objectification of the female body and celebrating the immense potential of women who, like birds, can soar above their adversities:

>There is
>a bird inside me
> it knows
>that my chest
>is not its cage.

The youngest poet in this collection, Swapnajita Sankhua is bold, assertive and allusive and writes with the assuredness and self-possession of a millennial, expressing her unstoppable youthful energy and enthusiasm in writing poetry:

>One day I started writing poems
>about the moments of dreams
>and their disruption,
>and became a rollicking river
>without fear of getting lost…

On the other hand, there are some young poets who are fiercely political, whose radical and revolutionary voices resonate through a searing indictment of the current social malaise - the perils of globalisation, social displacement, farmer's suicides, and crass consumerism. 'Tiger' is a plea to save the endangered animal, rueing that it is humans and not the tiger which are on the brink of extinction. The politically assertive 'Country' mourns the ineffectuality and impotency of the intellectual in instilling values in a fast-changing, corrupt society:

I have no guns, no bombs, no spears.
I have no weapons to protect anyone,
I only have my pen, my brush
And my restlessness.

Some like Madhuri Panda are filled with messianic zeal to ameliorate the condition of women. The poet finds strength in the power of words to effect dynamic societal changes and rouses women to a state of awakening in 'A Time to Speak out':

I'll light lamps of words
in every house.
How can I remain silent
when am I steeped in words?

Some of these poems reflect a deep concern with the role of an artist in society. It is interesting to note that an anthology where the contributors are not, strictly speaking, professional poets (although many one of them are recipients of literary awards at the local or district level) their deep understanding of the vocation of a poet, her ability to create or her being trapped in woefully hamstrung condition; is quite perceptive. Sunanda Pradhan realistically looks at the figure of a poet, shorn of all romanticism. She exhorts the reader to enjoy the creative piece and not to attribute its exquisiteness to the poet because:

Maybe, when you see him
your passion for poetry

may crack
like an eggshell.

It is interesting to note that the poet here is the figure of a man. Subhashree Lenka too describes the poet in 'Once You've Donned the Poet's Garb' as a male persona, engaged in the frenetic sphere of professional activity:

Once you have donned the poet's garb,
you forget the restraints that circle you;
you forget wife, son, daughter,
the heaps of files on the office table,
and the boss's angry face.

One wonders if this is inadvertent or a conscious choice on the part of the women poets or if it is the result of the translator's intervention since pronouns are gender-neutral in Odia language.

On the other hand, Pratidhara Samal's 'Poetry' describes poesy both in Romantic terms of enchanting the writer to "pull me out/ from abysmal depths" and in Arnoldian sense of discharging its function as an agent of social change, "it has the power/ to change the meaning of life-/whether in anger or in love." Many poems are about the search for the creative soul that is simmering beneath the toiling self and then finding a poetic voice and fructification. In a sudden burst of inspiration, while engaged in banal household chores, a young poet describes her creativity as a caged bird , which on its release , beautifully :

Flies
flaming a million lights
splitting the turbulent dark

The language of the poems ranges from the simple and direct to allusive and complex. Some of the poems are rooted in the soil as it were, earthy and realistic, while others are heavily laced with tropes and figures of speech, suggestive and imagistic, as if "to name is to destroy, to suggest is to create". The translator, the reader may note, has retained some of the names of the foliage in the vernacular, which richly contributes to the olfactory and sensory experience. 'Born a Woman' is a simple and plaintive cry about women suppressing their innermost feelings and desire but Srustishree Nayak takes recourse to rich, evocative and metaphoric language in 'Home' to depict a weary woman trapped in domestic drudgery yearning for an idyllic spiritual home. A veiled comparison to a soul's quest and its realisation of the futility of nurturing the corporeal frame is reminiscent of the metaphysical poet Andrew Marvel's ' On a Dew Drop' which equates a fallen dew drop's longing for self-extinction with the soul's desire to escape the world. Just as the self- contained fallen dew drop strives to shun contact with its surrounding petal, symbolising the contaminated world, and strains heavenward because of surface tension, the soul in Nayak's poem curls up within the body to free itself of its bodily prison:

>I wonder whose home is this one
>That I've been propping up
>All these years
>With my blood and sweat?

Many poems are replete with similar rich figures of speech and are interspersed with startling similes, metaphors and symbols. One such poem suffused with multi-layered allegory is 'Ahalya' which employs rich poetic devices such as annotation, connotation among many other. Lenka's 'The Hand' and Sunanda Pradhan's 'Holi' weave a rich tapestry of metaphors equating physical love with spiritual and are imbued with Sufi-like mysticism which envisages God as a lover. 'Sunlight' renders a

woman's fractured identity and thwarted aspirations through supremely elegant metaphors when she complains of her non-fulfilment to the man:
> You could have given me
> a cool full moon night,
> but since I asked,
> you tied to my sari end
> a handful of latticed sunlight.

The lines further go on to connote her splintered identity when she finds this dappled " sunlight escaping from my sari/ and getting strewn all over the floor/ like handfuls of rice." There are many other stylistic literary devices such as the alliterative lines of "fervour of flight to the fatigued fledgling" and the intriguing chiasmi as in "May be all that gives me pain /is the truth/ and all the truth you want to hide/from me is a lie" which contribute to the embellishment and enrichment of the poems. It goes to the credit of the translator who dextrously creates rich and unobtrusive images, managing to convey the sensation that one is reading the poems in the original language. These comparisons are woven seamlessly and effortlessly in the poem, sans artifice or forced contrivance.

The poems in this anthology are rich and variegated. They are not bound by an overarching theme, rather, the reader will find herself confronting an entire gamut of feelings and sentiments. Das has carefully curated this selection for the reader to appreciate the evolution of Odia women's voices spanning half a century and offer a mosaic of wide-ranging subjects, kaleidoscopic images and diverse experiences. Each poem is atypical and defies pigeonholing. Even though a common denominator running through them is a certain preoccupation with the position of women, their experience of love, loss, longing and desire, their finding of identity to come into their own; the poems go much farther to offer philosophic ruminations on the vagaries of life; on the infinite possibilities of death and salvation. Ultimately, they go beyond the generic issues restricted only to women and question the meaning of life, mourn the absence of healing power in this world and express existential angst, as in the location-unspecific, geographical boundary-transcending 'Chess Board', resonating in its depiction of transnational, universal misery, culminating in a heartfelt, metaphysical cry:

God!

Can you be trusted?

I know, there is no answer to this.

Readers desirous of learning more about the genealogy of women writing in Odia may refer to the scholarly introduction to *Antahpurara Abhilekha: Madhyakālina Nāri Prativā* (2015) where Sudarsana Acharya, Bhagyalipi Malla and Gouranga Charan Dash have discussed in detail the context in which women in pre-colonial Odisha composed their works.

J. P. Das translated the first thirty-seven poems in the volume with Arlene Zide (1940–2021).

References

J.P. Das and Arlene Zide. *Under the Silent Sun: Oriya Women Poets in Translation.* New Delhi: Vikas Publishing House Pvt Ltd ,1992.

J.P. Das. *In Other Words: Poems by Odia Women Poets.* New Delhi: Authorspress,2017.

Sudarsana Acharya, Bhagyalipi Malla and Gouranga Charan Dash. *Antahpurara Abhilekha: Madhyakālina Nāri Prativā.* Bhubaneswar: Odisha State Museum, 2015.

My Whole Life For Him
Manorama Mahapatra (Biswal)

If ever he comes under a silent sun
dampening my eyelids
or else in a heavy downpour
of the month of *shravana*
in the *behag raga* of the *sarangi*.

How would he know
I am not here any longer.
I burn like a wound
on some missile range by the sea.

Surely he would come.
The *neem* tree would have flowered,
Its fragrance drifting all around.
He'll grope for a lost childhood,
Will mope over it.
He won't have forgotten
That childhood like a squirrel's back;
The village childhood
Full of *neem* and mustard flowers.

A quiet girl like a shadow
Red-hued like the *manjistha* blossom
A sullen sunset in her eyes
Will ask about me
And other things.
But how would she know
For whom
A whole life passed,
Waiting, waiting.

So Many Days
Bijoyini Das

Where were you all these days?
In which forbidden world?
In which coveted heaven?
In which sealed fort of the heart?
Suddenly, today, you came.

Had I known that you would come
I'd have strewn your path
With flowers of myriad languages
Washed your feet in the holiest of water.

Tell me, which *Ganga* is holier than tears?
And which flower of a purer white than love?
Not finding anything else
I would have spread before you
My vanity
My arrogance
And my ego.

Placing your feet on these
You would have stopped awhile
And my centuries of waiting
Would have been transformed into *Ahalya*
With that momentary touch.
The lifeless skeletons of a thousand births
Would have sprung to life, become voluble.

But today, coming on you so unexpectedly
I have turned lifeless.

This is not the first time you have come.
Many times, in many forms you came
Just as I'm about to fall
You lift me up, re-tie the jingling anklets
Round my feet so I can climb,
Give voice to my mute lips.

Then, my intoxicated eyes
Covered by some far away illusion
Did not recognize you.

Sometimes, in coyness
I avoided you
Thinking of you as my love.
Other times,
Imagining you as God
I kept my distance,
Devotionless, detached.
But, for you, my love
Has been transformed

Forever, into an eternal garment.
What would have happened,
If you'd come a little earlier?
Would the mountains have melted?
Would the rivers have flowed in reverse?
The sun and moon, clasping hands,
Come down to Earth?

My life
On a track of its own
Would certainly have taken some other turn.

Ask Me
Bijoyini Das

Ask me –
How does it sound when the heart breaks
How, on a broken violin, a scale sounds –
Sa re ga ma ...

Ask me –
The meaning of hurt
The colour of that blood
Which turns from red into a deep black,
The smouldering incense of pain
Creates a fistful of the ashes of experience.

What music haunts
The casuarina trees of a ruined Konarka
The fossil of what dreams lie
Beneath the earth at Mohenjo-daro?
Ask me.

Is life just the other name of death
Living, deception;
Happiness, only hearsay;
Trust, the imagination of poets?
No, about these, don't ask me.

Coincidence
Jyotsna Das

When you meet the ocean
Your desires turn to waves
Words vaporize into air.
Taking a step forward
Your anxious thoughts flame into a pyre,
Wet feet and sand washed clean.

When you meet the forest
Your desires become the seasons
Your smiles turn into brooks
Thorn and brush drag at your feet
And the hills stop you on your way.

But, of coincidence pain is born.
Coincidence is happiness.
The camel resting on the desert sands
Rises, slowly moving
Towards a sudden liberation.

The eyes' tears
Cross the shores of the lips.
Dreams lie asleep
In closed rooms.
You wouldn't want to wake them
From the depths of slumber.

Dharmapada
Yashodhara Das

He did not have in his hands
Chisel and hammer
To crown Konarka
He is not Dharmapada:
In his hands
Is only a rickshaw handle,
Sheikh Khalil his name.
In those hands, thin as the *louki* vine,
The handle of a cycle rickshaw.
His legs still unfamiliar
With rickshaw pedals
Unafraid of trucks and buses
He drove the rickshaw
From Tulsipur to Jhanjirimangala.

Hands that should have held paper and pen
Hands that should have held the reel of a kite
Hands that should have held brush and palette
Hands that should have held a flute
Those hands held the handle of a rickshaw.
Unafraid, he pedalled
Ten hours a day
The entire burden of his family
On his shoulders.

How could head or hands
Tackle anything but the rickshaw?
Earning ten rupees
he could buy rice and dal,

Barley for an ailing sister,
A *burqa* for his mother,
A woman, unallowed
To work outside the home
She said to her son:
It's a man's duty to look after women.
Since his father ran away
From the battlefield of life
This twelve-year-old now heads the family.

Sheikh Khalil understands nothing.
This much he knows
He has to fix the crowning stone
On Konarka temple
With blood and sweat
Dragging his rickshaw
From Tulsipur to the OMP crossing.

Murderer
Mamata Dash

Did I ever call you?
No, I don't think so.
But then,
Where did you come from, and why?
Suddenly blackening
The heart of those bright days I'd earned.
The long, shining knife in your hand
Pointing only at me.
I know then it's only you who are my murderer.

Let it be.
To make this unbearable life of mine
Which gradually grows hotter
Worth living
I kept rearranging it all the time,
In all these,
From the constantly ending rainfalls
To the kiss which vanished in a moment
To the bed of snow which melted, in a moment.
But then, had I wanted
Somebody to murder me this way?
When I am so mauled, defeated
At the hands of unfulfilled aspirations?
Have you hung around your neck
That garland
Of all the faces that I loved, once called my own?
Then you've killed
The cuckoo's call, the moonlight, the honey,
The enchantment of my world.

The serpent's dance,
Killed the music of the flute
Echoing in my secret forest.
Purple blood sticking to your knife
The power of your presence shook
The very ground beneath my feet –
The drama of my past
Shines in the mirror of your crown jewel,
You laugh, laugh on and on
My head bent
In shame, in fear, devotion
Or is it the assurance of my having final shelter?

I won't go anywhere, I promise,
So do not bind my hands and feet,
I don't know where
This anxious wish comes from,
This yearning for the touch
Of your shining knife
This harsh touch of intense cruelty.
Look, something like a soft twilight
Surrounds us.

Come, murderer,
Step into my sacred courtyard
You're my last guest, after all, aren't you?
Come, today I feel, you also are my final love.

On My Own Grave
Banaja Devi

On my own grave I place a flower
Every day.
In the light of the early dawn
I tell the rising sun
Look,
Look, the lonely person loving you
Today is turned to stone,
So,
Only she deserves
The first ray of your rising glow.

On my own grave I place a flower
In the light of a midnight moon.
Seeing that spreading moonlight
I say,
Look,
Look, this lonely person loving you
Today is silent,
Among your scattered treasures
This, her silence
You alone deserve.

To The Bird
Banaja Devi

Say, bird!
Are you a raised eyebrow of eternal dawn?
A knife of light, sharp, ready to strike?
Always the adversary
Of ignorance, darkness, bondage?

Holi colors scattered
In the span of your soft wings.
A vibrance is in the air,
Flowers open their petal windows
And life flows into the lakes
Of delicate green grass.

You hand out invitation cards on gold-coloured paper
Tearing corners off gilt envelopes
Drops of fragrance scatter
Summoning anxious footsteps
When the finger points to the horizon.

Say, bird!
Are you a magnanimous emperor
Your treasure house of wealth unique
Sculpture and art beyond compare
Your nest hanging
Under this thin canopy of clouds.
The beauty of your hesitant wings,
Tired, folded up.

Magician
Shakuntala Devi

My noon blazed as in the blistering month of *Baisakh*
How damp it was, how warm.
Like a writhing fish near the banks
I opened my spider eyes and peered from
The distant window.

The heat, the blazing sun
Suddenly silent on the lonely island.
The morning's multi-coloured butterflies
Fluttered about, laughing
Chanting hymns of sacred moments.

When noon arrived they became drowsy,
Shrunken with fear,
Seeing me in this new guise.

A flower said, how do you feel
And dropped to the ground
This life took on new form
Midday turned to afternoon, then evening
Opened up the net
And one by one, threw away the fish.
From my window, the furrow of memory lengthened
The sun departing in the sky,
The half-light half-shadow of the world
I became trapped in my own amazement.

Before Anyone Comes
Pravasini Mahakud

Before anyone comes, I will return
As the daybreak, as a garland of dewdrops,
To morning's first step I will come
On gentle feet
Restless with impatience, to the waiting earth.
To light I move from darkness
I want to be the light.

Before anyone comes
I want to be a voice lost
In the chirping of the birds
Wipe the sun's scent from their wings
Drench them
In a bouquet of blessings.
Let's see if, just like that I can beat my wings
I am a lonely bird flying the empty blue skies.
Making no conditions, ready –
I declare my presence.

Before anyone comes
I am willing to be a river,
To quench the thirst of the entire world
Willing to be a tiny stream
In fields green with paddy
Where the farmer's whole year of dreams
Is suspended, searching the sky.

If another Buddha were to descend,
Releasing a thousand doves of peace

From the cruel hands of a barbarous Ashok,
Proclaiming love from his pitiless heart
In the place of war,
I might become the banks of the river Niranjana,
The shadow of the Bodhi tree.

Before anyone comes,
I am willing to be a torch
If the coming morning's path ahead is brightened
By erasing miles and miles of darkness.
From this time on,
I might become a seedling,
If, some years from now, of even a single wayfarer,
My shadow might ease the weariness.

I might spin a cocoon
Before anyone comes,
And after a few days, become a beautiful butterfly,
If children in a future garden
Ran to catch me on their tiny feet,
Drowning the cackle of birds with their sweet babble.
I might become a kite
To be flown through azure skies.
I might become a flower,
In the garden of time, the whole year long,
Become its pollen, become the fragrance
In its honeyed petals.

Before anyone comes,
I might become a canvas.
There'll come an artist who will paint on me
With all the colours of his heart,
The greatest picture of the 21st century.

Become a mountain of words,
A never-ending stream of passion,
For some poet-storyteller who will write
Life's epic.

Before anyone comes,
I might become Mother Mary or Devaki
And give the gift of Jesus and Krishna
To the world.
I might become a sky
Without the threat of star wars
Stronger than a thunderbolt.
For that man suffering in disease and pain,
I might become a honeyed, gentle touch.
Wherever I am,
No matter how far away,
I'll return,
A dream of the future.

Father
Pravasini Mahakud

Why didn't you kill me that very day, father
With your double-barrelled shotgun?
Why didn't you pull the trigger?
That day, the first time that I disobeyed you,
Talked back to you with bitter words?
I never had the confidence
To stand up to you.
The more you showed your love for me, the more
I hurt you. Why is that?
You've never slighted
My little whims, my wishes.
Never have you forced on me
The red whip of your will;
You always have been lenient.
So perhaps that's why I've done
Whatever I have wanted, for so long.
In the green forests of your trust
I'm an unwanted seedling.
And still cannot understand the reason why
Daughters such as I
With fathers such as you before them
Commit such wrongs.

Don't Know Why
Pravasini Mahakud

I live in your love
I die in your love
I burn and light others like a candle
Like the forest fire on either side.
I hear no one's call
The casual conversation of love and deception
Burdened with a sweet ache.

What is this feeling, this sweet sound
Which within me, shatters like glass?
This pitiful shivering? What is this poet's life
Heavy with defeat, steeped in loss
And the sadness of pleasure?
If I die now
Sorrow cannot lay its hand on my thick hair,
My closed eyelids, my lips, the garland of tears
My only consolation –
Once, I had taken out the man inside you
Holding his hands in the moonlight of affection.
I could make the man inside you
Stand under the shade of the *gulmohar* tree
In the season of flowers
In a tender spring
In a one-time love
You are that fully fulfilled need
I am a woman who goes on burning within herself
Who with the sound of a glass heart breaking
Shatters, shatters….

Wherever You Are, Whichever Way You Go

Pravasini Mahakud

Here I am, waiting for you like this
Not knowing which way to turn.

I don't know how long I'll stay this way.
Except for your address,
Except for the pain of our first meeting
You left nothing behind.
Not anything from which I could discover
Over and over again
The greatest gift of life.

Here I am, flashing on and off, off and on
A hundred-watt bulb of self-confidence
In the irritation of a power failure
In an inward-gazing grey sorrow
All alone in a hazy solitude.

Not for a moment did I ask for a promise
Nor did you give any.
Rainbows and moonlight,
Who doesn't need them?
But I can find my way
Through rain and moonless night
All these days, for this alone
I waited for your call.

Millions of times
I've come face to face with you

On another blue planet
The core of your being
Radiating a divine light
I'm covered in a rosy sweat
Of anticipation and excitement.
Year after year,
My confidence in meeting you even once
Secretly kept growing.
Today, without conditions,
Without hesitations,
My entire past present future
My complete incompleteness
And the inner conflict
Of desire and passion, yes and no –

These, I stand ready
To dedicate to you.

The Last Man
Sanghamitra Mishra

Am I the last man
Ramakrishna, Jesus, or Shankara
For whose coming such pitiful prayers are made
To gods on the shores of the ocean of milk?
For- whom sixteen thousand *gopinis* are born?
At whose wishes the monkey army
Is born to bridge the seven seas?

I am the last man
At the end of the line, sad and pallid
With empty sack and torn bag
Standing in line
Returning home disappointed when the shop is closed.
I am the last man within the four walls of this house.
Even if you sweep out all four corners
Here there is no sign of life.
Yet, breath keeps ticking
With the rhythm of the hands of the clock.
I am the man at the foot of the steps,
My eyes cannot find the sky above.
If I strain to see,
Time and time again, the heavy load slips off
I cannot straighten up my lowly head.

For that last man
The voiceless pain of waiting
When will he reach the Liongate –
Of the Jagannath temple

When will he beg benevolence of the god
At the end of the journey?
Of many beginnings, that is the end,
The proof of many hypotheses,
Of many ordeals by fire, the resolution.
The enchanted acceptance
Of many inevitable moments.

Though he is the last man
Wait and see
In three hours
The ration shops will open their doors
They'll throw wide the gates to the movie house.

Sorrow
Sanghamitra Mishra

Sorrow is the money-lender
Who sits on the doorstep.
You keep on repaying,
But can never pay it off.
It keeps mounting
Day by day.
Is there no escape?

He tries to jump over the circle
But only breaks his bones in a fall
In the race.
It is sorrow which sprints ahead of you
And reaches the goalpost first.

Sorrow is the goldfish,
Beautiful to behold in your net
But when you try to catch it
Slips away.

It is sorrow which waits for you,
At the door, like your mother.
Sorrow sits near the *Garuda* pillar,
Its fragrance wafts below the throne of God.
Omnipotent sorrow!

We, the humble subjects
Of its kingdom.
And for those it loves, sorrow makes its own
For them, it worries more than death.

It doesn't care if you are father,
Son, friend, wife.
In its reign, day and night are equal.
A perpetual deluge, a twelve-month monsoon,
An uncontrollable stream.

All eyes have lost their lustre
Sleepless, without food, burdened like a donkey.
Numberless sighs pent up within their chests
They are the subjects.
For them, the royal words are joyful,
Sorrow the only obedience,
Another name for life,
And history tells a tale of sorrow
Its colours fast, growing deeper every day.
Yashoda scatters a handful of rice
Before the sacred crow,
So he'll return.*

---

* *There is a belief in Orissa that if the crow caws you can expect a guest.*

Time's Other Name
Sanghamitra Mishra

Time has no name no caste
No parents no friends
It has no identity
Its footfalls are heard
In the beggar's bowl.
Time swings from the bird's nest
Time has gone with grandma's last tooth
Time laughed in the toothless mouth of the toddler
Time nods its head
On grandpa's brass headed walking-stick.

Like the resonance within the words
Like the picture of a man reflected in a mirror
Time looks at
You or me
How casually!
Time looks at *avatars* and prophets
In the fixed look of Urmila, Yashodhara
Time rings the last bell at school
When your heart pounds before exams
Time pats you on the head like your mother
Time stares with Yashoda's eyes
At the dust left by the chariot heading for Mathura.
The mother's heart is tired
A million knots are tied
In the unending string of waiting.
So who is it that divided time
Into three parts: past, present, future
Black and white get mixed up sometimes, like twins –
You can' t say who is younger, who older.

Time grew old
The day you propped up that creeper
Trampled under the cow's hooves.
In the noon sun
You opened an umbrella overhead.
When I sat dejected
Why did you make my mind stray?
Because you desire it
The chariot moves on Time's *badadanda**
The holy *salagram* stone rolls down
The waters of Gangotri
Because you want it so
Glass turns into gemstone
You'd like to wait
For the return of another deathless moment.

* *The main road in Puri leading to the Jagannath Temple.*

The Sea
Yashodhara Mishra

There is no escape from the sea.
Sometimes,
When you're not watching
It snatches things from your hands.
Sometimes, at your feet
It washes up
The things you'd thrown away.

Or, those cheap earrings
A little girl, bathing in the sea
Once had lost,
Had grieved over,
And, in the end, forgotten—
The sea washes up again,
After an age.

Midnight Train
Yashodhara Mishra

Waiting for the midnight train
Surrounded by mounds of sundry holdalls and trunks,
Nodding, wakes up with a start.
Checks his watch,
Becomes alert,
Stretches.
Lights a cigarette, paces up and down
Sees the people
Huddled in sleep
And smiles to himself.

Not yet time for the train to come.
The cigarette is finished,
The huddled people sleep on,
Not turning over even once.

Surrounded by mounds of sundry holdalls and trunks
The man checks his watch,
Nods off.

Untitled
Aparna Mohanty

What do you see
Looking at me like this?
Checking whether or not I resemble
Poetry's muse?
With which ornaments bedecked,
In what style my hair arranged?
If I'll sparkle exactly
Like that doll in your imagination?
Perhaps that thought has brought
A new glint to your eyes
Or
Undressing the coy maiden
In your mind.
You drag me to that temple of love.
The bridal chamber
The pen slips
Describing breasts and hips
Thoughts become
The lolling tongues of desire.

God!
From birth I've been brought up
In the blind well of ignorance,
Small-mindedness,
Happy always
To have offered into your hands
This rare womanhood,
My touchstone body
For weighing,
For your judgement,
Like some fresh-cut piece of meat.

I've kept quiet
I've accepted
That it's my nature
To keep quiet,
Even if I have no other
Respectable identity
But that of ovary
Approved by you.
That I can think, can feel,
That a special touch of the soul
Can redeem my frame of flesh and blood,
Can claim *paramarth,* the supreme meaning
Can achieve the *moksha* or salvation.
That this body is not
A silk-clad statue
Or a fly caught in a spider's web,
That this body can lift its head
And tower like a sky-touching temple
Of knowledge and consciousness,
Often waking to this possibility
In raised voice saying this aloud
I've stopped, from some odd fear
Kept silent,
Even though much earlier
Should have spoken out.
I would have said,
Addressing you alone –
Take off your mask,
Off with it!
What sort of friend are you?
What sort of soul-mate?
What kind of companion?
What kind of partner in life's journey?

Shame on you!
From history's beginnings
I have had to take as men
Carnivorous dogs and tigers
Shackled in the chains
Of rank and status.
Shame on me!
Unable to say this openly
Imprisoned in some enchantment,
Entangled in illusion.

So with bent head
I listen always
To my own suppressed and pitiful cries
Shame on me!
A hundred times more so than on you.
Feeling that this is all that I deserve,
Believing myself to be
The lowliest of the low,
Giving myself over
To the accursed half of the world.
Shame, and shame again!
On me
A hundred times more!

The Drain
Brahmotri Mohanty

It casually bears many shortcomings,
It is not in its nature to collect things;
Its achievement is in carrying things off.
Many new things come in new looks, new shapes,
It stirs them all up
And destroys the uniqueness of each.

We try to mutilate it,
Make it loathsome, ugly,
Slapping stains all over it
But that's just for a moment,
It humbles us,
Reasserts itself in its original form
The way it was a moment back.

We turn up our noses, but it is our own,
It never shames us, we die in our own shame.
What hope of gain? Do our interests clash?
It makes us feel small
And becomes great in its own right.
I bow before it,
But it's a bowing to my own senses.
Does the busy sun pride itself
At the greeting of the morning?

Good News Bad News
Giribala Mohanty

I'm telling it the way it happened.
This is the way the world is now.

Disease sorrow hunger in every house,
At the end of the month of *magha*
If it rains it's good for the king
Good for the land.
But this *magha* the heavy downpour
Wreaked havoc
The winter crop damaged,
Disease in every house.

And here, before month's end
Your pay packet finished.
The rations too.
Shortages everywhere.
It'd be a shame
If spring came now.
What would it think
Seeing such disease, such poverty, such sorrow?
Straining to feed a hungry belly
Who has the time to welcome it
With the melody of the *gundakeri* raga?
Where is the space
To write a welcome message
Or lay out a spread?
At the foot of a tree, on the footpath,
At the bottom of a drain, on the office veranda?
These are not fit places
For a visit from the prince of seasons.

Wherever You Are
Giribala Mohanty

Wherever you are
In the Kremlin or in California
In Berlin or Ethiopia
In Koraput or Korea
In plenty or in poverty
In famine or whatever
You are in,
It won't leave you.

It has no shame
It's not going to listen at all.
Whether this one is a socialist
Or the other, an imperialist.
Whether this one is a landlord
And that one just a farmhand.
It won't look at anyone's face.
With enormous force
It will devour you
Will burst out of you
To gobble you up.

It has a huge yawning mouth
Huger even than Koraput or Ethiopia
Than old age and disease
Than even Death itself.
Furious and fierce.
Though you have repeatedly
Not accepted it
Since it's insignificant, and vulnerable

It will call your bluff –
It will swallow you
And the whole world too.

It's the ferocity of the belly –
Hunger.

Woman
Giribala Mohanty

How can a girl child
Have anything like sorrow?

How can you be afraid
Of someone who you were born to,
Grew up with, travelled with?
Who you lived with
And will die with?
What's all this fuss about her?
How can a girl child
Have anything like sorrow?
That there' s all this commotion over her?

A mere woman
What's all this hope and yearning about?
You' re this man's daughter, that man' s wife,
That man' s mother. Stay that way.
Why should you go looking for a separate name?
You've been born, that's enough.
What is all this –
Feeling, needing, understanding?
How can a woman have a heart that throbs?
Take this offering.

There's this throne,
This altar on which gods are kept,
Give your all there, your offerings.
How can you expect some kind of return?
Ordinary desires, passions? – What of them?

You have to stay a goddess
Always shining in patience
Even as Kali, scimitar and skull in hand,
Killing the demon,
There's got to be a smile on your face!
How can there be anything like anger?
What is this curse?

You Forgot That
Giribala Mohanty

When you took me out to show me a mountain,
you forgot
That you yourself are a mountain
The heart may break
But you do not break.

When you took me out to show me the spring
you forgot
That you yourself are a spring
The tongue lolls with thirst in a gaping mouth
But you do not stop.

When you took me out to show me a temple-god
you forgot
That you yourself are a god
Knocked upon the stone in prayer,
the forehead cracks
But you do not budge.

The Pedlar
Nirmala Mohanty

The pedlar of happiness
Basket on his head,
Hawks his wares, his voice
Overflowing into the streets
Of Vrindavan, Mathura and Dwaraka.
The leafless *Kadamba* tree has budded
And the water ripples
In the Yamuna of the mind.

Who are you, pedlar?
Where is your home?
What is your name?
What pleasures have you brought to sell,
That, lusting after, I rush in and out of this house,
Like a madwoman.

Tell me the truth, pedlar
You're not going to cheat me
In the name of happiness?
My life's strings are bound
To the four walls
Sorrow its relentless fate.
I am but a basket of that sorrow,
A verse of despair.

I am a respectable woman, pedlar
I have crossed the threshold
And now stand
Upon the streets

Leaving behind family and caste,
My rank and honour.
At the magic of your call
I've run out
Into the open.

My straying feet won't return home, pedlar.
Honour once damaged, cannot be repaired.
When a dream palace is shattered
As when a glass doll breaks, it can't be fixed.

What spell then have you cast
That I go running blindly, after you?
What *raga* are you singing
That shakes the very soul
And jolts the universe?

Hold on, pedlar,
I will buy all the happiness in your basket,
At the price of my mind,
Paying for it with my grief.
I might lose everything in this deal,
But then who cares?
Let our bargain,
This profit and loss
Live for ever.

I Knew
Nirmala Mohanty

I knew you wouldn't come
Riding a magic horse,
A fairytale prince.

I knew you wouldn't bring
Golden deer, silver lilies
To please me.

Though hidden there on your silent lips
Are secret hints of promises
You won't express them.

My happiness, sorrow, laughter, cries –
You will not be a partner
Sharing in my journey's path.

Though strength resides
in your powerful arms
You're not the one to rescue Ahalya
With a touch.

My endless waiting meaningless, I know.
Then, spending time like pocket change
With what hope,
Why do I wait for your return?

After so much thinking
After realizing so much

Yearning stretches out like railway lines
As if there's so much more.

I feel, you are more than any of these,
Even more unfathomable,
Beyond compare.

Wife/Mistress
Sasmita Mohanty

1. Wife

In the posture of surrender
A peaceful, still, full river
Laughingly bears
The brunt of paddle and oar,
Is not troubled by
The ocean's fearsome roar.

In the courtyard
A small well
Full with sweet cold water
Whenever you need it,
There to quench your thirst.

2. Mistress

Rippling
Jumping, running
Over thorny ground
A tomboy brook
Its destination
Far away
Far, very far . . .

On the carpet of the grassy lawn
Slowly
Gathering
Drops of dew

Alluring as a diamond
Dazzling, but
Adds oil
To the fire of thirst.

Tomorrow
Amiyabala Muni

Tomorrow has promised
To come here
Riding the soft wings of a dove.
It will surely come here
As the auspicious promise
Of all my hopes.

It will enter my ill-fated life
And then . . .
Taking me as its own in a flood of affection
Will draw the rights to my existence
Into an everflowing stream.

Then, in my humble voice
I'll tell it
Wash away all my faults
In the purity of the scriptures
Accept me
Into your forgiving, loving pages.

My Mother is Smiling Today
Sulekha Samantaray

My mother is smiling today
My mother is smiling.

Today the fragrance of *Dussehra*
Spreads on the Autumn wind.

Today the stream of joy flows
Through the lanes and hamlets, the suburbs
and the cities.
The *kashatandi* flower is bent in laughter
And the *sunajhari* blossoms flutter to the ground,
Making everybody's face bloom
With a star of pleasure.

My mother is smiling today.
My mother is smiling.

Dussehra Is forbidden to me.
I am denied even simple laughter.
But who would dare deny me
The love of my mother
Who could part her from me?
Who could take from me this pen
Of tears?

Placing the only thing I own, my only treasure
At my mother's feet
I plead with her today
I worship her.

She goes on smiling, laughing
Sitting on her pedestal.

I go on watching my mother,
And she, me.
Suddenly my tears
Turn into pearls
And like some long-lost treasure
I collect them all
Carefully place them
In the storehouse of my grief.

Then, like blue and red lilies
In every corner of my mind
A wave of pleasure blooms and dances.

My mother is smiling today
My mother is smiling.

Rain Comes
Sarojini Sarangi

In the anxiety of
Excited moments
Of anticipated time and date—
After ruminating over
Sighs and dialogues
From the parentheses of meeting
I no longer wish
To lose myself , like a hermit
In a blemished forest;
I no longer wish
To lose myself like a shell
In the ocean of your eyes.

The postscript to
Love and many beliefs
Raises a voice of ending.
In the flush of my existence
The *Kadamba* flowers of love wither
In the embrace of crucified time.

The rains come in the month of *Baisakh*
Rain cascades through the blood in my veins
Rain comes leaping
Over the *Krishnachuda* tree of my restless age
In the warm breath of the century.

The Falklands
Pratibha Satpathy

In the water that eyes cannot reach
A slice of green full of life
In the branches thick with leaves
The restful nest,
Innocent leaves dancing in the breeze,
Reverberating with the chatter of young birds
Mankind's eternal land
The Falklands . . .
Where did all this fire come from?
From where the stretching of these pointed claws?
These sharp teeth?
Now then is only black smoke
Only blood—
Is this the blind vulture's greed?
His ruthless pride?
Say, you who ordains the fate of this world,
Look,
At all this charred green
This ravaged, bleeding nest
Look,
How, stretching out his wings
The bloodthirsty, blind vulture within you
Has blotted out the entire sky.

Heroine
Pratibha Satpathy

Listen
At others' hands, never.
At my own hands
I suffer torment
I become a net
Myself become bound up, entangled
Suffer.

Criticism, infamy
Plaintiveness, anxiety
I invite all of these upon myself
Cruelty, deceit
The bluff of lies
I leap beyond.
The five elements of life blossom
Blood flows unchecked
The surge of that river of blood
Washes away
My existence.
Still in my finest clothes
I envelop
This throne
Encrusted with precious stones.

Man—
Sometimes beggar, outcaste
Sometimes sovereign king
Or else, sometimes
An inspired hermit—

Out of his own desire,
Stands
Nearest to this throne.

I am supreme miserliness
Am ultimate charity
In a single point
The problem and its resolution
Like unquiet happiness
From a bleeding wound
Priceless
Myself the mystery
Myself the highest virtue.

A great poet
Is born
From every utterance
From my sidelong glance
From smile, from stance
From wounds, from joy
From arrogance, from anger
Even from my
Cruellest jealousy.
I am heroine, a *prima donna*
Without equal
Against destruction-seeking Time
I dare.

The Oyster
Pratibha Satpathy

In the empire of salt water
Ashamed, helpless
Before the yawning mouths of whales
My fate was just to keep on crawling.

You don't remember
The affinity of time.
Sometimes, at the crest of the ocean
A bright star shines.
Out of a million stars,
Why does just that one
Stare at me alone?
Or, is it
That I have, all on my own, called it mine
And offered to it
All the silent prayers of my heart?

From beyond the seven layers of the ocean depths
Someone calls
Come, get up, look at the sky!
A lightning strike within me.
The core of my pitiful body,
Smaller than the palm of your hand
Awakens.
Lips part.
From a great distance, from the sky
What is it that falls, succulent
A beauty never seen before?
A jot of creative imagination.

The void shakes.
Earth and heaven chime with a lilting *Om*
The entire sea rolls and sways.

Nearer and nearer
Comes the celestial drop,
It falls into my open mouth.
At that very moment,
In the green forests of romance
My new youth blossoms;
The next moment,
Becomes pregnant.

Eclipsed Time
Pratibha Satpathy

I feel as if I'm half-asleep
When what cannot be seen
Takes shape before my eyes
As if I'm in a long, dark cave
The desire to return, defeated
The body, a gradual anxiety
Of future allurements.

Once you've gone some distance
You can only look back,
And then a heart of stone breaks into sarcastic laughter
The one who laughs, invisible.
The mind, numb with despair
The long walk, for nothing.
The restlessness of the wound, alive.

The afternoon feels like a winter dawn
Dull yellow sun like the pallid glance of a sick moon
The lonely cawing of a crow
Like the cooing of the *Kumbhatua* bird
Are deceitful turns of phrase
Here hunger is inevitable
Food dear
Salt water for your thirst
And polluted air in every breath.

Mother-love here
Is a convoluted arithmetic of gain and loss
What other relationship is there?

In a night of famine
Numerous jealous ·eyes jostle you
Selfish hands are the swaying hoods of snakes
In totally false commiseration.
Awake, or sleeping
If you're not watching.
Your own kin become killers.

Day after day the serenading of the failed flute
Paints a dark shadow across the face
Imprints on body and mind
The ten thousand names of despair.

The Tryst
Sunanda Tripathy

When the whole city is asleep
I remove my anklets
And enter your room
On soft, stolen steps.

You lie there in your room
On the disordered bed, unmoving.
Books strewn all around.
In the midst of these, alone, you lie asleep
A smile of some strange contentment
On your sleeping face.
Quietly, by your bed, I sit
Smooth your dishevelled hair,
Then, bend down and with my sharp nails
Tear apart your chest
And with both my hands scoop out
A fistful of pulsating soft pink flesh.

By the odour of that flesh I am spellbound
Hold it to my breast.
They become one, for a moment,
The word and the silence
Then, they become one—
Sky and earth.

Before you wake
I put it back in place
Caress your open chest.

The wound fills up in a moment
As if nothing had occurred.

As before, you go on sleeping
Quietly, I walk out of your room.

Poem in Motion
Sunanda Tripathy

There is some ash, some blood
Sticking to the wings,
A dove flies
Around a ring of fire.

The people there
Mill around
Dressed in paper clothes.

Here youth falls
With the winter leaves
While someone signs a deed of compromise,
Reading the marks
Beneath someone's low cut neckline,
Another runs off.
Here youth falls with the winter leaves.

At the muffled cry
Of the ruined walls
The deep slumber
Of winter nights shatters.

The man on the street
Drags you to his alley
Where last night someone
Burnt down his hut.

While I was away
Time slipped under the door
A sealed envelope
I am afraid of opening.

The Sweet-Smelling Earth
Sunanda Tripathy

How can I prove it
when I myself don't know
If I am chaste,
unchaste?

Even so,
When the spell is broken
You'll see
On our village burning ground, my death fire
Reduced to cinders
The windswept ashes of my pyre blown away.
And the earth there
Being kissed
By a flock of butterflies.

Mirror
Bhagyalipi Malla

It makes them all its very own,
exactly as they are –
looks, form, tears,
odds and ends, fate and futility,
and the curse of the evil gods.

Every time I make up my mind
to get away from the mirror,
I find it ahead of me,
throwing everything back at me,
sending me back time and again
to my own darkness.

Now, I cannot encounter my own face.
I only see renunciation
and get a glimpse of the exile
in the hermit's hut.

When I ask the mirror
to tell me about myself,
it keeps silent,
confirming the truth
that reflections and images
are forever mute.

The Summit
Bhagyalipi Malla

The untold dreams in the skies, the river,
the silence, the snow-hewed flowers,
the unmindfulness –
you have settled yourself on them all
turning your back
on sound and time.

Sunk in renunciation,
hiding behind false mirrors,
you hold on yet to your countenance
and the fickle mysteries and passions.

Wherever you look,
there is only a bleached image
of an imagined past.

You have placed yourself in a corner
where the sky meets your solitude,
and where life is torn
between renunciation and rejoicing.

Hide And Seek
Bhagyalipi Malla

If you hide yourself,
I'm not sure I would ever find you.
You are always looking for ways to hide,
like the moon lost sailing into a stormy night,
like mountain peaks hidden behind teary eyes.

But where can you hide yourself?
The earth doesn't have darkness enough,
nor the flower space on its petals.
There is no space on the bee's wings,
or in the scarf of the breeze,
or in the lushness of the trees to hide you.

Give up the game of hide and seek.
Take away my vision if you can
and let the charade end.

Stay wherever you wish.
I would close my eyes
and get over my eternal dread
of losing you in the dark.

Farmer's Song
Chirashree Indrasingh

1
Awake all night
the farmer separates
grains and birds
from the ears of corn.
By morning,
paddy bags are stacked up
in someone's granary
as chirping birds
look for beakfuls of darkness.

2
We have a day marked
to celebrate the festival
of sowing paddy.
That day,
we disallow honeybees
to go on leave.
That day,
we spin yarns from sunshine
and fashion a sari of our choice
blending the clouds and
the lightning and the wind
and the festivities.

3
Unable to repay his loan
a farmer of our village
swallowed pesticide.
That should have been
the end of the story.
But his mother was seen
going round lamenting
that the bottle of honey
she had saved over the years
to treat the children for cold
was gone with him too!

That Night
Chirashree Indrasingh

I do not remember
if that night
there was a moon
or it was dark.
But I know you were there.
I didn't see
if there in the garden
flowers had blossomed or not.
But, since you were there,
I had transformed myself
into a tree of countless flowers
with a heavenly scent.
That night,
amidst the swarm of moths
you were there;
and I was a green forest
made of a million moths.
I am not sure
if you were there that night;
but that night,
I had confronted
all my stark passions
alone, by myself.

The Blue Saree
Sucheta Mishra

I have a blue saree that I wear
for the wedding of my friend
and the funeral rites of my neighbour's wife
who died a mysterious death.

Sometimes I take it out of the closet
to air it in the sun.
It is moth-eaten
but I keep on darning and repairing it
for I have to save it to bear witness to
many more sorrows and insults.

My lover writes to me
praising my blue saree,
but that too is a lie,
for all that he sees in it
is only flesh and heat and sensation.

I treasure my blue saree
to wear while standing beside
the wedding altar of my friend,
and the charred body of my neighbour.
They say I look special and beautiful
in that blue saree.
But I know
that it is only a piece of skin
which I'm clutching at
over the flesh and blood
of the woman's body that I've been given
forever to be debased.

Love
Sucheta Mishra

Don't try to tell me what history is,
for I know that love is greater.

I have seen edifices
standing on firm foundations of history
crumble and fall,
as I have also seen the tiny seed,
lost in the crevices of stone slabs,
grow into a full-blown tree.

If you look for them
there are instances galore in history,
but love does not need crutches
of instances.

With its million fingers
love takes out the greenery from darkness
and weaves a strange bond
with the bird perched on the tree,
as also with the man, axe in hand,
standing under its shade.
The bond outlives the bird which has flown
and the tree felled by the axe.
Hungry folks in their search
Are elated to see twin leaves sprouting
from the split trunk of the fallen tree.

They think it's a miracle, and, so
they write that down on the pages of history.

Boon
Swapna Mishra

I gave you freedom.
I gave you the boon
to disappear
in the skies
like the illusory cloud.
The dried flower bud
between the pages
of the old diary:
I gave you a lovely garden.
The moon rising
over the eyelids:
I gave you the river bank
and the expanse of sand
which you always wanted.

I gave you moonlight.
I became blind.

Darling Daughter
Swapna Mishra

My darling daughter!
Don't look up at the sky;
look below at the earth.
Oh! how easily you obey.

Look at all the blood
in the skies.
The evening is giving birth
to an eternal night.

Some day,
when they dredge
this civilisation of ours,
they will surely find
your tear drops,
still fresh.
The fossil would reveal
how cruel the world has been.

No flowers bloom
in the garden;
our breathing
is bereft of air.
Don't keep searching.
Forget all you know:

Don't look at the skies,
don't look at the earth.
Face the endless depths

beneath your feet.
Darling daughter,
accept the reality.

A Time to Speak Out
Madhuri Panda

You ask me to be silent,
but how can I, at this time?
I have just finished making
the flowers of words bloom.
Some were jealous,
some threw mud at me,
some others put me on the dock.
But then,
some picked up the flowers too.
I had nothing to call my own,
but I'm happy that all my secrets
are now in the open.
If you have a grenade in your hand,
I've love in my heart,
and I know
that nothing matches its colour.
How can I then be silent
at a time like this?
I'll light lamps of words
in every house.
How can I remain silent
when I'm thus steeped in words?
I'll make even you eloquent.

Till Then
Madhuri Panda

Our tears we drank as if nectar.
Did fate destine us for such darkness?
We had nothing more to say to each other.
We were destined to stray
and we got lost.
Our days passed in indifference,
but myriad changes have occurred since.
People have built their houses
in villages wiped off by cyclone,
and have regained their faith.
The girl who had run away
is back home, three months gone.
The uproar over Radha goes on.
The sky remains the same.
Nothing more has happened to us.
The fire which had scarred our dreams
continues to burn us.

Listen to what I say from my heart:
I say that everything will change.
Crossing the barbed wire fence,
I'll come back wearing the blue sari
I had saved from another birth,
and, we will resume our talk
from where we had left off.
And, yes,
the word you searched for restlessly
to end your poem with,
I promise you,
I'll come as that lost word;
I'll surely come again.

In Silence
Sharmistha Sahu

Your unseen hand
knocks on the door
and I dissolve
beyond the body's walls.
There is turmoil
in the garden.
The flower of life
is breathless with fragrance.
How many times shall I tear apart the webs of illusion,
and
look for blood-soaked light in the ocean of tears?
Let the communion
of the closed door
fall silent.
Let me not return
to the confines of my body.
let you materialise
before me,
this moment.

Flight
Sharmistha Sahu

There is
a bird inside me;
it knows
that my chest
is not its cage.
It sings
as it flies;
it bewilders me
with its many guises.
It keeps flying
severing relationships,
tearing apart intimacies.
It flies
flaming a million lights,
splitting the turbulent dark.
Because it flies
I am limitless.
I keep scattering the wind,
but it does not run out.
How futile of you
to keep measuring me,
appraising the shape
of my eyes, nose and lips!

Chiaroscuro
Sharmistha Sahu

Is my love
part real, part illusion?
How terribly lonesome I am
on this path!

The leaf that trembles
hesitant on the tree,
my heart which flutters
at my own footfall –
be silent and stand still.

I have stolen the light
from the distant horizons
of my mist-ridden journey.

My mortality is my beauty.
My loneliness is my strength.

I am surrounded
by the grey eyes of dusk.
The ultimate confessions,
written with my blood,
suffuse my inner being.

You stand there
beyond the moments
of light and shade.
Could I possibly
call you my own?

Shower at Sunset
Subhashree Lenka

The shower at sunset
washed the dust from the leaves,
whisked away the remnants
of tenderness from the petals,
swept away the layers of pollution
from the sky's expanse,
and,
gave back the fervour of flight
to the fatigued fledgling.
The shower at sunset
opened the doors of the house
lying locked and neglected for ages
and shattered its silence.
It stepped unto the darkness
of the abandoned place,
where lay trapped in time
emptiness, loneliness
and many forgotten passions.

The tremor of the droplets,
in enchanting whispers,
sent out the message of dreams
and flowers and scent and magic
and of close intimacy.
The shower at sunset
made us remember
to get drenched all night long,
and to drift like a piece of straw
in the fast flowing stream
of passionate yearnings.

Come this Night
Subhashree Lenka

This night
in her star-studded brocade saree
looks as if an ever-youthful angel,
bewitched by the earth,
has chosen to descend.
There is a fragrance in the air
and a fire in the breath
and faith flows like a lost river.
Wings take butterfly hues and wait
to fly unto the petal the dust of moonlight.
This, my body of five elements,
turns into a temple
to welcome the beloved one in a redolence
of camphor, sandal and incense.
It seeks to swim
in the river lost in mist and dew;
it wishes to warm up
the secreted desires in a simmering fire.
Come this night
in a vapour of musk on your body.
Hold me captive in your supple arms.
Come in the sound of anklets
on your lotus-red feet
and trample on the slumber of my body.
Come with the thirst
of living in your drunken eyes;
come with the burning flame of passion
in your thirsting lips.
Let's then, the two of us,

like birds searching for honey in flower dust,
sing to every pore of our bodies
the hearty ditties of pleasure.
Let blood, marrow, flesh, nerve and bone
keep awake all night long.
Let the water drops on lotus leaves breathe
eternal life unto the slumbering moments.

Come, let's together shatter
the utter silence of this night.

Once You've Donned the Poet's Garb
Subhashree Lenka

Once you have donned the poet's garb,
you forget the restraints that encircle you;
you forget wife, son, daughter,
the heaps of files on the office table,
and the boss's angry face.
Your thoughts stretch out like a kite string
enticed by the far horizons.
The surrounding noise abates.
Your feet grow cold,
and a wintry soft loneliness grips you
though you're in the midst of a crowd.
In times like these, the poet leans
on his pen, his only friend.
Sometimes he strains and struggles
to capture the words eluding his grasp;
at other times,
reposed on the throne of his chosen words,
he caresses the poem with a paternal touch.
In the heavenly garden,
swaying like a divine flower,
decked-up ideas and expressions
come floating, exuding fragrance
in rolling waves of poetry.
The poet loses himself in his own creation.
After the pangs of creation,
the poet gathers his gains and returns
to his own intimate circle.
And as soon reverts

to being father, brother, flunkey
till such a time
as he might don the poet's garb again.

Woman
Subhashree Lenka

Earth
You dig and plough her,
and she offers you food;
she braves cyclones and quakes
and stays calm.

Water
Drawn from well and river
she gives life to the thirsty.
A sword can't split her apart.
She bears all her scars
as if writ on water.

Air
Scents sweet and foul –
she envelops all in her graces.
Good and bad –
she shelters them all
with her benign goodness.

Fire
She burns eternally
in the lac-house of pain
to emerge as pure gold;
even though consumed
by the fires of body and mind.

Void
Everyone her own
she hands out affection,
intimacy, love
with a generous heart;
even as she hides
within her limitless bosom,
as wide as the open skies,
all the sound and fury
of thunder and lightning.

Your Hand
Subhashree Lenka

Soft and warm
like the dove's breast
your hand touches me all over,
wipes off my loneliness
and washes me with your
sandal-scented intimacy.
Holding your hand,
I walk and cover far distances
in difficult terrain
in a flitting moment.
Your hand shows me the way
in the darkest night
even as it sweeps away
obstacles from my path
before my feet touch the ground.
Sometimes your hand
pats me on the back, lovingly,
as I drift between mid-dream
and unfulfilled wishes
and my straying eyes close
and I slide into a deep sleep.
Your hand caresses
the unruly tresses falling on my face,
wipes off the drops of sweat,
and relieves me
of all my silent, secret sorrows
and all my tender laments.

Poetry
Pritidhara Samal

There is someone inside me
who is looking for poetry
all the time.
But then, poetry is not a ladder
which you climb up
to touch the skies.
It's not a boat to go across
the seas of life and death.
Poetry is the tumult
of unending silence inside me;
it's the enchanted feeling
which is at the same time
both helpless and all powerful.
It's a weapon
which cannot alter fate and future,
but it has the power
to change the meaning of life -
whether in anger or in love.
That's the reason
I seek out poetry.
Poems pull me out
from abysmal depths;
give me support like pillars.
Poems pave for me a golden path
clearing my mind of rubbish.
Poems fill me up
with multiple manifestations
pushing away my wailing griefs.
When a feeling dies inside me,

they blow through me
like a fresh breath of air.
It's said
that poetry tells lies
and fabricates false dreams.
May be,
but it has also become my very own
and blessed me with solace.
It has stood by me like a shadow
when everyone has forsaken me.

Sunday
Pritidhara Samal

I had many plans for today:
to invoke lost relationships;
to nurture the seedling
fashioned out of the night's darkness;
to water the flower pots;
to spruce up my living room
with a handful of morning light;
to gather a drop of dew from the grass
and secrete it in the jewel box.
I freed myself from my burdens
and resolved that:
I'd scrub off the dirt and dust
gathered on my body;
I'd rescue my mind from neglect;
I'd remove cobwebs from dense times;
I'd tidy up my house
from the anarchy of disorder.
But nothing got done.
Before I could make up my mind
from where to start,
someone walked past my house.
I heard a lonely wail
as if from the eternal void.
A wounded joy assailed me.
The roaring ocean stood still.
My shadow lengthened and vanished.
I drifted like a boat
into the blue river of the past.
A lost smile alighted on my lips.

I had got nothing done today.
But then, imagine,
how successful and meaningful
the day had been for me!

Chess Board
Pratiksha Jena

Under whose ruthless orders
are some people getting displaced
leaving behind hearth and home
and the identity of their ancestors?

They tie up in bundles
the sweat saved over the years,
broken pieces of living,
and a handful of dust
from the wilting golden harvest.

At the same time
some people are taking over
through trickery
the treasures of heaven
and the lost keys of a golden citadel.
And, gleefully decorating
their palaces, courts
and their chess boards of deceit.

God!
Can you be trusted?
I know, there is no answer to this.

Ahalya
Pratiksha Jena

I wish to turn into stone
for once.

Once did I wish for something
and doors had opened
and the forest had vanished.

In my greed,
I had gathered a potful of false affections
mixed in sand and grit.

Tell me,
what curse grows on that fertile soil now.

I had collected from the dark chamber
a handful of faith
which now fades in the sunlight.
I did not know that,
nor did you.

Look,
numbness creeps up my feet,
my thighs and my waist
and the layers of memories of your body.

One seeks to put together
the broken pieces of the mirror
and cook and serve on a leaf platter
the two restless eyes snatched by magic.

An island sinks mid-ocean,
and, I slowly turn into stone.

Sunlight
Pratiksha Jena

You could have given me
a cool full moon night,
but since I asked,
you tied to my sari end
a handful of latticed sunlight.

As I undress,
I find sunlight escaping from my sari
and getting strewn all over the floor
like handfuls of rice.

There is sunshine, the colour of fish,
in the warm breath of the two shadows
holding hands in the virgin embrace
of the dark night.

Burn me down if you wish
in a blazing fire.
Let sunlight drip off my body
in droplets of sweat.

Truth Untruth
Ipsita Sarangi

I do not know the art
of converting lies into truths.
I do not know what makes it
a truth or a lie.
May be all that gives me pain
is the truth,
and all the truth you want to hide
from me is a lie.
I had proclaimed from the house-tops
that I would speak the truth
and nothing but the truth,
but it was an empty boast.
In the end, I was as lonely as ever.
Can one lay himself open to truth
the way he wants?
I didn't get what I wanted
or, may be,
I wanted much more than I got.
May be all that I thought was right
turned out to be all wrong.
The shadow that stands
across all truths
is a hand that points at the truth,
and is the answer
that will resolve all my doubts.

Born a Woman
Ipsita Sarangi

You have to spread out
your existence
to the two extremities
of the horizon.

You have to turn your eyes
away from the demands
of body and mind
and paint on your lips
a perpetual smile.

You have to persuade yourself
that you can live only when
you keep your sulk hidden
in some secret cavity.

Sometimes, your very existence
would seem to be
desolate as the skies;
your verdant dreams
would drop dead on the ground
in the swelter of unconcern.

After the swinging days
in the laps of flowers,
it is now your time
to be trapped in the petals
and go begging
for another breath of life.

If You Meet a Poet
Sunanda Pradhan

If you like a poet's poems
read them again and again;
learn them by rote;
remember them;
recite them to yourself
in the solitude
of open fields and rooftops.
But
never
Never try to meet the poet.
May be, when you see him
your passion for poetry
may crack
like an eggshell.

The poet's mind
may not be as beautiful
as his beautiful poems;
his heart might not beat
like a rippling stream
You may find him more common
than the common man.
Read the poem
and forget the poet
forever.
If you happen
to meet a poet
somewhere, sometime,
never seek to find in him
a poet's soul
or a lover's charm.

Holi
Sunanda Pradhan

If you wish
to splatter me
with colours,
come to me
in the silent hours
of the night,
after the city
has gone to sleep.
With your bare hands
smear the whole
of my body
with colours yellow
and red
and green.

Let the colours
ripple over
from my body
to my mind,
and from my mind
to my soul.

Let the colours
thwart cleaning
and stay fast
on my body.

Let a new day break
in virgin, vibrant colours.

To the Seashore
Sunanda Pradhan

Let's go
to the sea shore
for once
and look at the moon
sitting on the sands.

We'll sit in silence
side by side:
no words, no laughter.
We'll simply look
at the lonely moon.
The sea breeze
will pull at my saree
and touch me
on the earlobe,
and check my whole body.
And we'll sit there
quiet in the moonlight
for a few moments.

Time hangs heavy
and I'm restless.
Let's go
and look at the moon
on the sea shore.

Looking at the Sea
Sunanda Pradhan

I shall never
go to the sea
all by myself.

I like to look at the sea
in silence.
I like the cool breeze,
the beach, the moonlight.

But I do not
want the sea
in solitude.
I do not want its touch,
its trust,
and its faithlessness.

I know
that the sea
cannot be distrusted,
nor can you
put your faith in it.

It may take away
my remaining years
and my dreams.

Never again shall I go
to the sea alone
to be flung between
faith and betrayal.

Having lost
all my passion
and having distanced myself
from trust and faith,
and having given up
all my desires,
I shall never go
to look at the sea again.

Violence
Gayatribala Panda

There lies the handkerchief
soaked in blood.
It's the same one
I'd wiped my face with,
the same one I'd bought
for a mere ten rupees.

I had walked up the stairs in haste
wiping off the sweat on my face;
by the time I walked down,
the white handkerchief lay
at the bottom of the stairs
drenched in blood.

All those who went up the stairs
before I did –
did they all have red-hued sweat?
Did they all have a vaulting ambition
to attain fame?

There is no one else here.
Only me and my hunger.
Whose blood is this then –
of which bird or beast?

How does it matter to me?
Let me look over my hands,
my forehead, my clothes.
There is no blood there.
Why should I then worry?

Clouds darken the sky.
Let me take leave;
let me reach home
as fast as I can.

Tiger
Gayatribala Panda

The subject of today's meeting
is the decline
in tiger numbers
from countries, forests, and also from our
minds.
On this,
some expressed sorrow,
some were agitated.
Some others suggested ways
to increase the tiger population.
Some ascribed it
to the devastation of forests;
some put the blame
on man's excessive fear of tigers.
Some pointed their fingers
at industrialisation
even as some argued
that globalisation was the root cause.
Sitting at a corner of the back row
I imagined the lecture hall
to be a dense forest
and the speakers, each of them a tiger,
alive and abominable.
I pictured a tiger opening its jaws
when they spoke, their rant a wild roar.
When they gasped
I could make out a fiery pretence.
When they put forth their proposals
it was as if they were leaping at the

gallery
inviting the audience into their maws.
I sensed that as long as
the human population grew,
tigers wouldn't perish
Mobiles, phones and the Internet
will make tigers obstinate, arrogant,
ambitious
and they'd, in the twinkling of an eye,
reach the recesses of the earth
and touch the skies.

I saw tigers emerging
from mobile phones and laptops
and springing at us.
I could well imagine the big cats
holding condolence meetings
for the extinction of mankind.

Country
Gayatribala Panda

Where do I stand?
I have no guns, no bombs, no spears.
I have only a pen
and my imagination and my sorrow.

The words I picked up at random
and secreted in my room
suffocate me in my helplessness.

Some words, shot down by Maoists,
lie helpless in jungles and caves.
Some unknown words, placards in hand,
are on a sit-down strike.
Some words are making rounds
of courtrooms year after year.
Some words wait patiently
in the Panchayat courtyard
for their BPL cards and old age pension.
Some words seek to salvage their fate
in a surfeit of darkness after the rape.

I am in my room
surrounded by those words
amid blood and tears and pity and sighs.
I do not know what I should be doing
for my country.
The country belongs to those
who have muscle power, money
and it is they who worry about the country.
Or so they say.

Where do I stand?
My heart palpitates
if someone cries somewhere.
My confidence is shaken
when someone faces defeat.
When someone trips and falls,
it breaks my heart.

I have no guns, no bombs, no spears;
I have no weapons to protect anyone,
I only have my pen, my brush
and my restlessness.
I sit in my room surrounded by them
and write poems and paint pictures,
and shuffle about.

The words, the paintings and the people
I do not know what to do about such a land.
Even though it slows as blood in my veins
I do not know how to advise others
how to love this country.

No One Comes
Srustishree Nayak

No one comes;
why is then
this eternal waiting?

I sit open-eyed
and all agog,
my ears pricked up
for the sound of footfalls,
and my doors wide open –
but no one comes.

Years have passed
and I've continued to wait,
but the one
who had made the promise
has not turned up.

The lines under my eyes
are now darker;
passions have frozen;
emotions have turned to sighs.
In the fire of separation
love has turned into a handful of ashes.

But,
I haven't given up yet;
and I am hopeful still,
as I realize
that for one dedicated waiting
an entire lifetime
is indeed too short.

Home
Srustishree Nayak

I have lived in it for years
but haven't been able
to call it my own is
it really my home?

You said
it's my inheritance;
so, I've stayed on here keeping
the hearth burning,
rolling wicks for the prayer lamp,
nursing plants in the garden.
But when I sweep the rooms,
I find myself thrown out
with the garbage.

Nothing is ordained I know;
but I try to realize myself
within the confines of the four walls.
I take measured steps,
cautious of the door sill,
dreaming all the while
of living elsewhere.

But where is that home
the real life trapped in another?
Where is the secret home
that I've been building
within the other one?

I wonder whose home is this one
that I've been propping up
all these years
with my blood and sweat?
Whose is it really
when all my dreams,
my love, and even my identity
all lie elsewhere?

Beloved's Life
Prabasini Hota

She lives from moment to moment
amidst her strange fancies.
She keeps no measure,
but I quietly strike off the moments
from my own life count.
The mischievous wind, jealous,
stops a while to steal away
her fragrance.

I am humbled by her every word.
Does she understand
how it gives one life?
Her poems carry
the aroma of her love,
and I tattoo them all over my body
and silently pray
for adding to her years
the remaining days of my life.

I force the remaining strands
of happiness
out of my life even though
one life is not enough
to nurture another
with drops of one's tears.
With the belief that grass may grow
even from concrete floors,
I nurture no regrets.

Can one live a full life of one's own?
It's no small achievement
for a dreaming poet to live his life
which begins and ends
with a single poem.

To My Pallbearers
Subhashree Subhasmita Mishra

They interred
my barely breathing body
and went home.

They washed themselves clean
with soap and detergent,
in the steaming bathroom.
Poured water on the body
towelled themselves clean,
did absolution.

Their meal was my body,
my limbs the dishes
which they ate their fill,
and their body is now content.

They now went out in a procession
with placards that carried
the news of my violent death.

The mystery of all is that
I myself observed mourning,
wrote poems,
watched news on television.

The dead body and the pallbearers
had become one and the same.

Sentry
Sasmita Rout

I know the three best ways to reach God.

On the first road
a young deer kid is running away.
There is a dead body lying on the road
which is bustling with noise, and I am alone.
The road goes on and on and I return
to the spot from where the deer kid had taken off.

On the second road,
he was standing facing me,
and did not look as if he would be had easily
but I have faith in myself.
For me love is growing, under strain
far, far away.

I also know the easy and ultimate route
where I am standing guard since eternity
to tell the last man on earth
that there is a giant hole here.
Go back and look for a new road.

Deity
Sasmita Rout

If I could gather all the nights!
This night the sea didn't sleep a wink
as it had failed to return even a single anklet;
the night when my tresses lay like a dead fish
on my bare shoulders.

The night when a poet had splattered his tears
on a string of stars and said, 'Get lost'.
The moon was getting brighter,
and high above the sea just the two of us.

Time was taking long strides to run away
from some unknown melody chasing it.
It was the night when an artist had
hurriedly blew away the lamp.
But was he ever able to paint darkness?

The night when an assassin turned on the bed
looking at his double, asleep, clasping him.
If I could gather all the nights,
I'd still be left with a morning,
where someone would be wishing:
"Let the deity be safe and sound wherever he is"
It does not matter to us?

Colours of Words
Tanmayee Rath

What colour shall I give
to your anger and sulk?
What brush can paint
the language of your lips and eyes?

All the colours of the world
find their salvation in you.
There are no miracles
with which to compare you.
Flowers, and diamonds,
and pearls and gold –
they will all blanch in your presence.

I need no pilgrimage when
all the piety of temples and mosques
hover around you;
there I'll make an offering
of the delicate flowers of my heart.

Share a slice of your smile
for which the morning waits sulking.
The earth awaits your command to rain
to shower her with greenery.

You are my sage, my lover,
I'm ever lost in your depths.
Born as your beloved,
I chant mantras as I surrender to you,
worship you, fall at your feet,
my eternal lover.

Failed Assassin
Tanmayee Rath

Who knows what shape it'll take,
and what great transformation?
What brush can paint the eyes
which will make
the brightest point shine
with a sidelong glance?
Can you figure out
the hidden meaning?

Can you fathom the dagger point
sameness of pleasure
and renunciation,
union and separation,
surrender and love-making?

The conspirator draws
a question mark
on your delicate feelings.
Do you know
who perpetrates these pretences?

Behind the mask
surely lies the deep darkness
that pervades
the self-proclaimed viewer.

Let this be known
that they may die an apparent death
through your conspiracy,
but it is never their end.

Not today, not tomorrow
you can never ever do it
for you are a failed assassin.

Mask
Swapnajita Sankhua

In the hazy light
of pretence or love
I was continuing to lose
my existence.
You kept on sketching pictures
of sin and virtue on my body
which lulled me
to death and rebirth.

One day I started writing poems
about the moments of dreams
and their disruption,
and became a rollicking river
without fear of getting lost,

Stop me if you can.
Walk with me if you may.
Or if you are that lucky
become my destination.

I know you can't.
So, choose your own riverside
between doubt and deception
and look into the mirror of my bosom.
Failing to recognise yourself,
remove your masks
one after the other,
and, keep on looking at yourself.

Acknowledgements

I am deeply grateful to Shri J. P. Das for giving me an opportunity to edit this volume of poems that he has so painstakingly gathered and translated over the years. I am humbled by the trust he has reposed in me in editing and commenting upon the words that are so dear to him. My heartfelt gratitude to Shri Rajendra Kishore Panda for providing the bio notes of some of the contributors to this volume. My sincerest thanks to my friend and colleague Animesh Mohapatra whose aversion to my indolence and constant goading has always resulted in positive academic outcomes, as with the present enterprise. I am indebted to him for offering me a perspective on the tradition of Odia women's poetry and for sensitising me to the linguistic nuances of a language unknown to me.

- Vinita Gupta Chaturvedi

Notes on the Poets

Manorama Mahapatra (Biswal) (b. 1948) writes poetry, children's literature, travelogues, literary criticism, and essays. She was a Professor of Odia at Rama Devi Women's College, Bhubaneswar and received a Senior Fellowship from the Government of India to pursue research. She has received many awards; notable among these include the Odisha Sahitya Akademi award in 1998 for her anthology of poems titled, *Phalguni Tithira Jhia* (*Maiden of Spring*).

Bijoyini Das (b. 1944) has a Masters in Psychology. She has published seventeen books, including novels, short stories and poetry. A journalist, she does programmes for radio and television and is at present researching on Devadasis of Odisha.

Jyotsna Das (b. 1958) is an MA in Odia literature. She teaches in the Women's College, Rourkela. Her writings have appeared in various magazines since 1977. She has published a collection of poems and a novella.

Yashodhara Das (b. 1949) is the Managing Director of Diamond Telecomponents. She has published nine anthologies of poetry in Odia and two children's books in English. She has won many awards, some of which are the Best Poet award from Vishwa Odia Sammelan (2013) and Odisha Sahitya Akademi (2022).

Mamata Dash (b. 1947) has published nine anthologies of poetry, four anthologies of short stories, three essays, one novel and written an English monograph on Bhubaneswar Behera (Central Sahitya Academy). Some of the prestigious awards she has received are Odisha Sahitya Academy, Bharatiya Bhasa Parishada

National Award, Bishuba Award, Bhanuji Rao Award and Bharat Naik Smriti Sammana. She received senior fellowship from cultural department of India to research on Genesis of Radha.

Banaja Devi (b. 1941) has four collections of poems, five collections of short stories and five novels to her credit. She is a recipient of many awards, some of which are the Odisha Sahitya Akademi Award, Fakir Mohan Sahitya Puraskar, Istahaar Kabita Puraskar, Sarala Devi Smruti Puraskar, Gyanada Kabita Puraskar, Bhanujee Rao Kabita Puraskar and Manjari Devi Sahitya Puraskar.

Shakuntala Devi (b. 1945) is a prolific poet and has five collections of poetry to her credit. She is also the author of a novel, and a collection of short stories.

Prabasini Hota (b. 1981) is a teacher by profession and writes poems in both Odia and Sambalpuri. Her first poetry collection *Premikara Aakasha* was published in 2021.

Chirashree Indrasingh (b. 1966) has published three poetry collections, ten short story anthologies, and two novellas. She has received the Bhubaneswar Book Fair Award, Kanheilal Award, Subrata Rath Memorial Award, Sucharita Galpa Purashkar and a fellowship from the Department of Culture, Government of India. She has translated Namita Gokhle's novel *Things to Leave Behind*, Bhalachandra Nemade's novel *Koshla* (original Marathi) and Jayant Mahapatra's anthology of poems *Sky without Sky* from English to Odia.

Pratiksha Jena (b. 1974) is a well-known Odia poet and fiction writer. She has published six collections of poems and a novel in Odia. Her first collection of poems was published in 2014 by Sahitya Akademi under the Navodaya Scheme. Her poetic vision is essentially feminist, and she writes for human liberty and equality.

Subhashree Lenka (b. 1973) is a poet and social worker who currently heads the Sambad Sahitya Ghara, Odisha's largest literary organisation, as its state coordinator. Her publications include *Asha* (2005), *O* (2010), *Akashare Aji Janha Nahin* (2013),

English anthology *Nightscapes* (2016), *Sei Shabdamane* (2018), *Samayara Upakatha* (2021) and Hindi anthology *Apni Paridhi ka Akash* (2022).

Pravasini Mahakud (b. 1957) is a poet and a translator. She has a Masters in Odia literature. She has published thirteen poetry collections and has translated twenty eight books from Hindi to Odia. She is the recipient of the Odisha Sahitya Akademi Award, Jhankar award, Junior and Senior fellowships from the Ministry of Culture, Government of India.

Bhagyalipi Malla (b. 1965) has published several collections of poetry and essays in literary and cultural journals. She has received awards including the National Excellent Women's Award and Rajiv Gandhi Sammana.

Sanghamitra Mishra (b. 1953) is a Reader in Odia at Utkal University, Bhubaneswar. She holds a PhD in Modern Drama. Her work includes literary essays in modern drama and poetry. She has published a collection of poems.

Subhashree Subhasmita Mishra (b. 1982) has published several Odia poetry anthologies which include *Aranyaa, Agnikaa, Garbhagni, Agni Saraswati* and *Aayudhaa*. She is a recipient of several awards and honours, including Timepass Prathama Award, Timepass Bahibandhu Samman, Baragada Kavya Phaguna Award, Pallaban Shabda Samman and Kavi Samman. She has several books like *Aranya, Agnika, Garvhagni, Agni Saraswati, Aayudha* and *Himagni* (2022) to her credit.

Sucheta Mishra (b. 1965) has published ten anthologies of poetry, three novels, one collection of short stories and one collection of essays. She has received several literary awards including the Odia Yuva Sammana (1997) and the Gangadhar Foundation Award.

Yashodhara Mishra (b. 1951) has been a Professor of English under MP government; a visiting Fellow at Mason de Science, Paris; and a senior research Fellow of UGC and IIAS, Shimla. She has published short stories, novels, poems and travel stories and some of her writings are part of school and college syllabi. The literary awards she has received include the Sahitya Akademi award, Odisha Sahitya Akademi award, Katha award (Delhi), Odisha Book Fair award and Binapani Mohanty Puraskar among many others.

Aparna Mohanty (b. 1952) is a celebrated feminist voice in Odia literature. She taught Odia Literature at Tulasi Women's College and is at present professor-emeritus of Odia literature. She did her PhD on women characters in Odia fiction and has published three critical essays, seventeen collections of poetry and four translated works. Her work *Jhiapaine Jharka Tia* received an award from the State Sahitya Akademi in 2007.

Brahmotri Mohanty (b. 1934) has been writing poetry since 1956. She has written nearly five hundred poems, most of which have been published. She is the recipient of the Odisha Sahitya Akademi Award, 1985, and the Visuba Award of the Prajatantra Prachar Samiti, in 1962, 1976 and 1984. Her poems have been translated into English and Urdu.

Giribala Mohanty (b. 1947) completed her PhD from Visva Bharati, Santiniketan where she served as Professor and Head, Department of Odia. She has eight anthologies of poems in Odia, one in Hindi, nine books of criticism, a few edited works and four translated books to her credit. She is associated with organisations like Sahitya Akademi, Central Institute on Classical Tamil and National Book Trust.

Nirmala Mohanty (b. 1948) recently published two collections of poems. She has also published a collection of short stories and two volumes of children's literature. She has been writing since 1965 and her works have appeared in many journals, on All India Radio, and on television in Odisha.

Sasmita Mohanty (b. 1967) has been writing poetry since 1984. She also writes short stories and children's literature. Her articles have appeared in various Odia literary magazines and newspapers, and on All India Radio. She is the daughter of Nirmala Mohanty.

Amiyabala Muni (b. 1941) is the recipient of awards for three of her short stories and for one of her novels as well as two collections of poetry. Her writings are published widely in various Odia literary magazines.

Srustishree Nayak (b. 1977) has published a collection of short stories and an anthology of poems. She is the recipient of Sahitya Akademi Yuva Puraskar.

Gayatribala Panda (b. 1977) has to her credit nine collections of poetry, two novels and two collections of short stories. She has received the Sahitya Akademi Yuva Purashkar in Odia for her poetry collection *Gaon* and Rajiv Gandhi Sadvavana Award. She is the editor of *Anyaa*, an Odia literary magazine. In 2015, she was chosen for the Writers In-Residence programme at the Rashtrapati Bhavan. In 2022, she received Sahitya Akademi Award Odia for her poem 'Dayanadi'.

Madhuri Panda (b. 1971) has three collections of poetry to her credit.

Sunanda Pradhan (born 1976) has to her credit three collections of poetry, three collections of short stories and five novellas. She edits *Megha*, a literary magazine in Odia and heads *Ink Odisha*, a leading publishing house of Odisha.

Tanmayee Rath (b. 1987) works as a lecturer in Odia at Rairangpur college, Mayurbhanj. Her maiden book *Nilasammohana* was published in 2018. A recipient of Manthana Yuva puraskar for creative writing, Tanmayee writes both poetry and criticism in Odia.

Sasmita Rout (b. 1984) is a post-graduate in Botany from North Orissa University. Sasmita writes poetry in Odia and her first verse collection was published in 2018 in *Sanchar*. Her poems have appeared in newspapers and magazines such as *Sambad, Nitidina, Sailaja* among others.

Sharmistha Sahu (b. 1971) has published several anthologies of poetry named *Sukha Sabu* (2009), *Pabanara pacheri* (2013), *Jhadapakshira* gita (2016), *Rati jagualira daka* (2021), *Jhad pakshi ke* *git aur anya kabitaen* (Hindi translation, 2022). She has received numerous literary awards including Odisha Bahimela Sammana, Saptarshi Kavita Sammana, Lekhalekhi Yuva Kabi Samman, Sachchi Routray Nabaparba Kabita Samman, Kabi Basanta Muduli kabita puraskar, Kalinga Literary Award, and Time Pass best seller award.

Pritidhara Samal (b. 1973) is an Assistant Professor in Odia at Government College, Koraput. She has to her credit five poetry collections and a monograph on Ramakanta Ratha's poems. She has received several state level awards, including the State Youth Award from Ministry of Culture, Government of India for her poetry collection *Khela*. She is the Vice President of the oldest literary organization of Odisha, Utkal Sahitya Samaj and is a member of Odia Advisory Board of Sahitya Akademi.

Sulekha Samantaray (b. 1953) teaches English literature at SVM College, Jagatsingpur. A collection of her poems in English has been published. Her short stories and poems both in English and Odia appear regularly in journals.

Swapnajita Sankhua (b. 1998) is a political science graduate and a prominent new voice in contemporary Odia poetry.

Ipsita Sarangi (b. 1975) has published six collections of poems, one book of critical essays, and translated six works into Odia including a collection of Octavio Paz (published by Odisha Sahitya Akademi). She has received many awards including Odisha State Youth Award for poetry, State Youth Award, Utkal Mani Yuva Prativa Samman, Chausathi Yogini Pratibha puraskar and Basanta Muduli Smruti Samman.

Sarojini Sarangi (b. 1948) is an obstetrician and gynaecologist by profession. A collection of her poems has been published. Her poems and articles appear regularly in Odia newspapers and journals.

Purabi Satapathy (b. 1981) holds a bachelor's degree in arts from Utkal University and a Diploma in Apparel Designing. Her poems – on various themes including love, nature, mysticism, spirituality, and humanism – have been widely published in periodicals and on social media. Her poetry collection *Raga Poorvee* has been published by Sahitya Akademi.

Pratibha Satpathy (b. 1945) has a PhD in modern Odia poetry and taught at R. D. Women' s College, Bhubaneswar. She has published seven collections of poetry. She is a recipient of various awards including the Visuva Award for Poetry (1981), State Sahitya Akademi Award for Poetry (1986), Rastrapati Award in Bhopal, Rastriya Kabir samman (2017) and Saswati Rastriya Puraskar in Karnataka.

Sunanda Tripathy (b. 1968) is among the leading women poets of Odisha and works as a journalist.

J.P. Das (b. 1936) is a well-known Odia writer. He has published several volumes of poetry, short stories and plays. *First Person, Love is a Season, Timescapes,* and *Silences* are English translations of his poetry. He has researched on Odishan art and his scholarly publications include *Puri Paintings* and *Chitra-Pothi*. His novel *Desha Kaal Paatra* (published by Penguin in English translation as *A Time Elsewhere*) is a historical narrative set in nineteenth-century Odisha.

Arlene Zide (1940–2021) was a Chicago-based Professor of Foreign Languages. She co-edited ***Primavera***, a women's literature and arts journal published from Chicago. She lived in India for her research in tribal languages and was a Visiting Professor at Jawaharlal Nehru University. She published original poetry as well as translations in Journals in India and the US.

Vinita Gupta Chaturvedi (b. 1963) is an Associate Professor in the Department of English, Delhi College of Arts & Commerce, University of Delhi. She has done her undergraduate, masters and M. Phil studies at the University of Delhi. Her doctoral thesis on the British writer George Eliot was awarded by the University of Lucknow. Her publications include book chapters, articles and reviews in journals. She has recently guest-edited the May 2021 and December 2021 issues of the *Salesian* Journal, a publication of Salesian College, Siliguri.

Black Eagle Books

www.blackeaglebooks.org
info@blackeaglebooks.org

Black Eagle Books, an independent publisher, was founded as a nonprofit organization in April, 2019. It is our mission to connect and engage the Indian diaspora and the world at large with the best of works of world literature published on a collaborative platform, with special emphasis on foregrounding Contemporary Classics and New Writing.